mischievous mischievou

mischievous mischievou

mischievous mischievous

mischievously mischievously

mischievously mischievously

mischievously mischievously

muscle muscle muscle muscle muscle

muscle muscle muscle muscle muscle

necessary necessary necessary

necessary necessary necessary

unnecessary unnecessary

unnecessary unnecessary

unnecessary unnecessary

neighbour neighbour neighbour

neighbour neighbour neighbour

nuisance nuisance nuisance

nuisance nuisance nuisance

occupy occupy occupy occupy occupy

occupy occupy occupy occupy occupy

reoccupy reoccupy reoccupy reoccupy

reoccupy reoccupy reoccupy reoccupy

occupation occupation occupation

occupation occupation occupation

occur occur occur occur occur occur
occur occur occur occur occur occur
reoccur reoccur reoccur reoccur
reoccur reoccur reoccur reoccur
opportunity opportunity opportunity
opportunity opportunity opportunity
opportunities opportunities
opportunities opportunities
opportunities opportunities
parliament parliament parliament
parliament parliament parliament
persuade persuade persuade persuade
persuade persuade persuade persuade
sincere sincere sincere sincere
sincere sincere sincere sincere
sincerely sincerely sincerely
sincerely sincerely sincerely
soldier soldier soldier soldier soldier
soldier soldier soldier soldier soldier
stomach stomach stomach stomach
stomach stomach stomach stomach
sufficient sufficient sufficient
sufficient sufficient sufficient

insufficient insufficient insufficient
insufficient insufficient insufficient
sufficiency sufficiency sufficiency
sufficiency sufficiency sufficiency
suggest suggest suggest suggest
suggest suggest suggest suggest
suggestion suggestion suggestion
suggestion suggestion suggestion
suggested suggested suggested
suggested suggested suggested
forwards forwards forwards
forwards forwards forwards
extreme extreme extreme extreme
extreme extreme extreme extreme
experience experience experience
experience experience experience
earth earth earth earth earth earth
earth earth earth earth earth earth
early early early early early early
early early early early early early
describe describe describe describe
describe describe describe describe
circle circle circle circle circle circle

circle circle circle circle circle circle
build build build build build build
build build build build build build
breathe breathe breathe breathe
breathe breathe breathe breathe
answer answer answer answer
answer answer answer answer
address address address address
address address address address
actually actually actually actually
actually actually actually actually
purpose purpose purpose purpose
purpose purpose purpose purpose
probably probably probably probably
probably probably probably probably
pressure pressure pressure pressure
pressure pressure pressure pressure
possess possess possess possess
possess possess possess possess
tomato tomato tomato tomato
tomato tomato tomato tomato
tomatoes tomatoes tomatoes
tomatoes tomatoes tomatoes

fruit fruit fruit fruit fruit fruit fruit
fruit fruit fruit fruit fruit fruit fruit
grammar grammar grammar
grammar grammar grammar
occasion occasion occasion occasion
occasion occasion occasion occasion
occasionally occasionally
occasionally occasionally
occasionally occasionally
straight straight straight straight
straight straight straight straight
strength strength strength strength
strength strength strength strength
therefore therefore therefore therefore
therefore therefore therefore therefore
various various various various
various various various various
train train train train train train train
train train train train train train train
explain explain explain explain
explain explain explain explain
skate skate skate skate skate skate
skate skate skate skate skate skate

estimate estimate estimate estimate
estimate estimate estimate estimate
inflate inflate inflate inflate inflate
inflate inflate inflate inflate inflate
pray pray pray pray pray pray pray
pray pray pray pray pray pray pray
yesterday yesterday yesterday
yesterday yesterday yesterday
always always always always
always always always always
plane plane plane plane plane plane
plane plane plane plane plane plane
plain plain plain plain plain plain
plain plain plain plain plain plain
great great great great great great
great great great great great great
stayed stayed stayed stayed stayed
stayed stayed stayed stayed stayed
afraid afraid afraid afraid afraid
afraid afraid afraid afraid afraid
sleep sleep sleep sleep sleep sleep
sleep sleep sleep sleep sleep sleep
teacher teacher teacher teacher

teacher teacher teacher teacher
sphere sphere sphere sphere sphere
sphere sphere sphere sphere sphere
beard beard beard beard beard beard
beard beard beard beard beard beard
wheel wheel wheel wheel wheel
wheel wheel wheel wheel wheel
stream stream stream stream stream
stream stream stream stream stream
hear hear hear hear hear hear hear
hear hear hear hear hear hear hear
here here here here here here here
here here here here here here here
cleaner cleaner cleaner cleaner
cleaner cleaner cleaner cleaner
between between between between
between between between between
cream cream cream cream cream
cream cream cream cream cream
earn earn earn earn earn earn earn
earn earn earn earn earn earn earn
meaningful meaningful meaningful
meaningful meaningful meaningful

tearing tearing tearing tearing
tearing tearing tearing tearing
learning learning learning learning
learning learning learning learning
alive alive alive alive alive alive
alive alive alive alive alive alive
reptile reptile reptile reptile reptile
reptile reptile reptile reptile reptile
flight flight flight flight flight flight
flight flight flight flight flight flight
night night night night night night
night night night night night night
quiet quiet quiet quiet quiet quiet
quiet quiet quiet quiet quiet quiet
quite quite quite quite quite quite
quite quite quite quite quite quite
cried cried cried cried cried cried
cried cried cried cried cried cried
replied replied replied replied replied
replied replied replied replied replied
highest highest highest highest
highest highest highest highest
invite invite invite invite invite

invite invite invite invite invite
cycle cycle cycle cycle cycle cycle
cycle cycle cycle cycle cycle cycle
admire admire admire admire
admire admire admire admire
frightening frightening frightening
frightening frightening frightening
throne throne throne throne throne
throne throne throne throne throne
alone alone alone alone alone alone
alone alone alone alone alone alone
hoped hoped hoped hoped hoped
hoped hoped hoped hoped hoped
owner owner owner owner owner
owner owner owner owner owner
spoken spoken spoken spoken spoken
spoken spoken spoken spoken spoken
homeless homeless homeless
homeless homeless homeless
clothes clothes clothes clothes
clothes clothes clothes clothes
throat throat throat throat throat
throat throat throat throat throat

frozen frozen frozen frozen frozen
frozen frozen frozen frozen frozen
telephone telephone telephone telephone
telephone telephone telephone telephone
moan moan moan moan moan moan
moan moan moan moan moan moan
stroke stroke stroke stroke stroke
stroke stroke stroke stroke stroke
poached poached poached poached
poached poached poached poached
explode explode explode explode
explode explode explode explode
moon moon moon moon moon moon
moon moon moon moon moon moon
stool stool stool stool stool stool
stool stool stool stool stool stool
glue glue glue glue glue glue glue
glue glue glue glue glue glue glue
fruitful fruitful fruitful fruitful
fruitful fruitful fruitful fruitful
flute flute flute flute flute flute flute
flute flute flute flute flute flute flute
treasure treasure treasure treasure

treasure treasure treasure treasure

amuse amuse amuse amuse amuse

amuse amuse amuse amuse amuse

chewed chewed chewed chewed

chewed chewed chewed chewed

cruise cruise cruise cruise cruise

cruise cruise cruise cruise cruise

juice juice juice juice juice juice juice

juice juice juice juice juice juice juice

salute salute salute salute salute

salute salute salute salute salute

injure injure injure injure injure

injure injure injure injure injure

excuse excuse excuse excuse excuse

excuse excuse excuse excuse excuse

rabbit rabbit rabbit rabbit rabbit

rabbit rabbit rabbit rabbit rabbit

buzzer buzzer buzzer buzzer buzzer

buzzer buzzer buzzer buzzer buzzer

copper copper copper copper copper

copper copper copper copper copper

traffic traffic traffic traffic traffic

traffic traffic traffic traffic traffic

lesson lesson lesson lesson lesson
lesson lesson lesson lesson lesson
bubbles bubbles bubbles bubbles
bubbles bubbles bubbles bubbles
puddle puddle puddle puddle puddle
puddle puddle puddle puddle puddle
ladder ladder ladder ladder ladder
ladder ladder ladder ladder ladder
cannot cannot cannot cannot cannot
cannot cannot cannot cannot cannot
butter butter butter butter butter
butter butter butter butter butter
slipper slipper slipper slipper slipper
slipper slipper slipper slipper slipper
riddle riddle riddle riddle riddle
riddle riddle riddle riddle riddle
happen happen happen happen
happen happen happen happen
cotton cotton cotton cotton cotton
cotton cotton cotton cotton cotton
shield shield shield shield shield
shield shield shield shield shield
relieve relieve relieve relieve relieve

relieve relieve relieve relieve relieve

niece niece niece niece niece niece

niece niece niece niece niece niece

reindeer reindeer reindeer reindeer

reindeer reindeer reindeer reindeer

relief relief relief relief relief relief

relief relief relief relief relief relief

thumb thumb thumb thumb thumb

thumb thumb thumb thumb thumb

climb climb climb climb climb climb

climb climb climb climb climb climb

crumbs crumbs crumbs crumbs

crumbs crumbs crumbs crumbs

wrapping wrapping wrapping

wrapping wrapping wrapping

comb comb comb comb comb comb

comb comb comb comb comb comb

knight knight knight knight knight

knight knight knight knight knight

sword sword sword sword sword

sword sword sword sword sword

whisper whisper whisper whisper

whisper whisper whisper whisper

wreath wreath wreath wreath
wreath wreath wreath wreath
wriggle wriggle wriggle wriggle
wriggle wriggle wriggle wriggle
whole whole whole whole whole
whole whole whole whole whole
doubt doubt doubt doubt doubt
doubt doubt doubt doubt doubt
plumber plumber plumber plumber
plumber plumber plumber plumber
look look look look look look look
look look look look look look look
looked looked looked looked looked
looked looked looked looked looked
looking looking looking looking
looking looking looking looking
jump jump jump jump jump jump
jump jump jump jump jump jump
jumped jumped jumped jumped
jumped jumped jumped jumped
jumping jumping jumping jumping
jumping jumping jumping jumping
talk talk talk talk talk talk talk talk

talk talk talk talk talk talk talk talk
talking talking talking talking
talking talking talking talking
live live live live live live live live
live live live live live live live live
lived lived lived lived lived lived
lived lived lived lived lived lived
living living living living living
living living living living living
skipped skipped skipped skipped
skipped skipped skipped skipped
share share share share share
share share share share share
sharing sharing sharing sharing
sharing sharing sharing sharing
shared shared shared shared
shared shared shared shared
move move move move move move
moved moved moved moved moved
moved moved moved moved moved
moving moving moving moving
moving moving moving moving
bake bake bake bake bake bake bake

bake bake bake bake bake bake bake
baked baked baked baked baked
baked baked baked baked baked
baking baking baking baking baking
baking baking baking baking baking
doze doze doze doze doze doze doze
doze doze doze doze doze doze doze
dozed dozed dozed dozed dozed
dozed dozed dozed dozed dozed
dozing dozing dozing dozing dozing
dozing dozing dozing dozing dozing
pat pat pat pat pat pat pat pat pat
pat pat pat pat pat pat pat pat pat
patted patted patted patted patted
patted patted patted patted patted
patting patting patting patting
patting patting patting patting
drag drag drag drag drag drag
drag drag drag drag drag drag
dragged dragged dragged dragged
dragged dragged dragged dragged
dragging dragging dragging
dragging dragging dragging

pin pin pin pin pin pin pin pin pin
pin pin pin pin pin pin pin pin pin
pinned pinned pinned pinned pinned
pinned pinned pinned pinned pinned
pinning pinning pinning pinning
pinning pinning pinning pinning
bat bat bat bat bat bat bat bat bat
bat bat bat bat bat bat bat bat bat
batted batted batted batted batted
batted batted batted batted batted
bore bore bore bore bore bore bore
bore bore bore bore bore bore bore
bored bored bored bored bored bored
bored bored bored bored bored bored
boring boring boring boring boring
boring boring boring boring boring
atlas atlas atlas atlas atlas atlas
atlas atlas atlas atlas atlas atlas
atlases atlases atlases atlases
atlases atlases atlases atlases
minus minus minus minus minus
minus minus minus minus minus
minuses minuses minuses minuses

minuses minuses minuses minuses

cross cross cross cross cross cross

cross cross cross cross cross cross

crosses crosses crosses crosses

crosses crosses crosses crosses

argue argue argue argue argue argue

argue argue argue argue argue argue

argues argues argues argues argues

argues argues argues argues argues

ambush ambush ambush ambush

ambush ambush ambush ambush

ambushes ambushes ambushes

ambushes ambushes ambushes

studio studio studio studio studio

studio studio studio studio studio

studios studios studios studios

studios studios studios studios

wish wish wish wish wish wish

wish wish wish wish wish wish

wishes wishes wishes wishes

wishes wishes wishes wishes

speech speech speech speech speech

speech speech speech speech speech

speeches speeches speeches speeches
speeches speeches speeches speeches
branch branch branch branch branch
branch branch branch branch branch
branches branches branches
branches branches branches
virus virus virus virus virus virus
virus virus virus virus virus virus
viruses viruses viruses viruses
viruses viruses viruses viruses
miracle miracle miracle miracle
miracle miracle miracle miracle
icicle icicle icicle icicle icicle icicle
icicle icicle icicle icicle icicle icicle
cradle cradle cradle cradle cradle
cradle cradle cradle cradle cradle
particle particle particle particle
particle particle particle particle
candle candle candle candle candle
candle candle candle candle candle
rectangle rectangle rectangle
rectangle rectangle rectangle
crackle crackle crackle crackle crackle

crackle crackle crackle crackle crackle
example example example example
example example example example
cuddle cuddle cuddle cuddle cuddle
cuddle cuddle cuddle cuddle cuddle
buckle buckle buckle buckle buckle
buckle buckle buckle buckle buckle
agree agree agree agree agree agree
agree agree agree agree agree agree
disagree disagree disagree disagree
disagree disagree disagree disagree
honest honest honest honest honest
honest honest honest honest honest
grace grace grace grace grace grace
grace grace grace grace grace grace
disbelieve disbelieve disbelieve
disbelieve disbelieve disbelieve
healthy healthy healthy healthy
healthy healthy healthy healthy
unhealthy unhealthy unhealthy
unhealthy unhealthy unhealthy
true true true true true true true true
true true true true true true true true

untrue untrue untrue untrue untrue
untrue untrue untrue untrue untrue
pack pack pack pack pack pack pack
pack pack pack pack pack pack pack
unpack unpack unpack unpack
unpack unpack unpack unpack
fasten fasten fasten fasten fasten
fasten fasten fasten fasten fasten
unfasten unfasten unfasten unfasten
unfasten unfasten unfasten unfasten
frost frost frost frost frost frost frost
frost frost frost frost frost frost frost
defrost defrost defrost defrost defrost
defrost defrost defrost defrost defrost
part part part part part part part
part part part prat part part part
depart depart depart depart depart
depart depart depart depart depart
fuse fuse fuse fuse fuse fuse fuse
fuse fuse fuse fuse fuse fuse fuse
defuse defuse defuse defuse defuse
defuse defuse defuse defuse defuse
wrap wrap wrap wrap wrap wrap

wrap wrap wrap wrap wrap wrap
unwrap unwrap unwrap unwrap
unwrap unwrap unwrap unwrap
cover cover cover cover cover cover
cover cover cover cover cover cover
uncover uncover uncover uncover
uncover uncover uncover uncover
form form form form form form form
form form form form form form form
deform deform deform deform deform
deform deform deform deform deform
recover recover recover recover
recover recover recover recover
prevent prevent prevent prevent
prevent prevent prevent prevent
present present present present
present present present present
prepare prepare prepare prepare
prepare prepare prepare prepare
refill refill refill refill refill refill refill
refill refill refill refill refill refill refill
reform reform reform reform reform
reform reform reform reform reform

pretend pretend pretend pretend
pretend pretend pretend pretend
permit permit permit permit permit
permit permit permit permit permit
perfume perfume perfume perfume
perfume perfume perfume perfume
persist persist persist persist persist
persist persist persist persist persist
perspire perspire perspire perspire
perspire perspire perspire perspire
precise precise precise precise precise
precise precise precise precise precise
request request request request
request request request request
quickly quickly quickly quickly
quickly quickly quickly quickly
circular circular circular circular
circular circular circular circular
certainly certainly certainly certainly
certainly certainly certainly certainly
Scottish Scottish Scottish Scottish
Scottish Scottish Scottish Scottish
cabbage cabbage cabbage cabbage

cabbage cabbage cabbage cabbage
cocoa cocoa cocoa cocoa cocoa cocoa
cocoa cocoa cocoa cocoa cocoa cocoa
circumference circumference
circumference circumference
circumference circumference
crayon crayon crayon crayon crayon
crayon crayon crayon crayon crayon
colourful colourful colourful colourful
colourful colourful colourful colourful
cinema cinema cinema cinema
cinema cinema cinema cinema
scene scene scene scene scene scene
scene scene scene scene scene scene
cyclone cyclone cyclone cyclone
cyclone cyclone cyclone cyclone
garden garden garden garden garden
garden garden garden garden garden
gutter gutter gutter gutter gutter
gutter gutter gutter gutter gutter
golden golden golden golden golden
golden golden golden golden golden
goggles goggles goggles goggles

goggles goggles goggles goggles
going going going going going
going going going going going
geography geography geography
geography geography geography
generate generate generate generate
generate generate generate generate
giant giant giant giant giant giant
giant giant giant giant giant giant
giraffe giraffe giraffe giraffe giraffe
giraffe giraffe giraffe giraffe giraffe
guess guess guess guess guess
guess guess guess guess guess
orange orange orange orange orange
orange orange orange orange orange
digestion digestion digestion
digestion digestion digestion
magnify magnify magnify magnify
magnify magnify magnify magnify
ache ache ache ache ache ache
ache ache ache ache ache ache
echo echo echo echo echo echo echo
echo echo echo echo echo echo echo

orchestra orchestra orchestra
orchestra orchestra orchestra
anchor anchor anchor anchor
anchor anchor anchor anchor
chemistry chemistry chemistry
chemistry chemistry chemistry
choir choir choir choir choir choir
choir choir choir choir choir choir
scheme scheme scheme scheme
scheme scheme scheme scheme
elephant elephant elephant elephant
elephant elephant elephant elephant
phone phone phone phone phone
phone phone phone phone phone
photograph photograph photograph
photograph photograph photograph
alphabet alphabet alphabet alphabet
alphabet alphabet alphabet alphabet
nephew nephew nephew nephew
nephew nephew nephew nephew
apostrophe apostrophe apostrophe
apostrophe apostrophe apostrophe
which which which which which

which which which which which
profit profit profit profit profit profit
profit profit profit profit profit profit
prophet prophet prophet prophet
prophet prophet prophet prophet
beech beech beech beech beech beech
beech beech beech beech beech beech
piece piece piece piece piece piece
piece piece piece piece piece piece
peace peace peace peace peace peace
peace peace peace peace peace peace
threw threw threw threw threw
threw threw threw threw threw
road road road road road road road
road road road road road road road
rode rode rode rode rode rode rode
rode rode rode rode rode rode rode
rowed rowed rowed rowed rowed
rowed rowed rowed rowed rowed
helpful helpful helpful helpful helpful
helpful helpful helpful helpful helpful
truthful truthful truthful truthful
truthful truthful truthful truthful

wasteful wasteful wasteful wasteful
wasteful wasteful wasteful wasteful
skilful skilful skilful skilful skilful
skilful skilful skilful skilful skilful
beautiful beautiful beautiful beautiful
beautiful beautiful beautiful beautiful
thoughtful thoughtful thoughtful
thoughtful thoughtful thoughtful
grateful grateful grateful grateful
grateful grateful grateful grateful
deceitful deceitful deceitful deceitful
deceitful deceitful deceitful deceitful
mansion mansion mansion mansion
mansion mansion mansion mansion
confusion confusion confusion
confusion confusion confusion
emotion emotion emotion emotion
emotion emotion emotion emotion
action action action action action
action action action action action
decision decision decision decision
decision decision decision decision
comprehension comprehension

comprehension comprehension
comprehension comprehension
objection objection objection objection
objection objection objection objection
addition addition addition addition
addition addition addition addition
direction direction direction direction
direction direction direction direction
education education education
education education education
subtraction subtraction subtraction
subtraction subtraction subtraction
laundry laundry laundry laundry
laundry laundry laundry laundry
caution caution caution caution
caution caution caution caution
audience audience audience audience
audience audience audience audience
faulty faulty faulty faulty faulty
faulty faulty faulty faulty faulty
Bible Bible Bible Bible Bible Bible Bible
Bible Bible Bible Bible Bible Bible Bible
horrible horrible horrible horrible

horrible horrible horrible horrible
invisible invisible invisible invisible
invisible invisible invisible invisible
responsible responsible responsible
responsible responsible responsible
central central central central central
central central central central central
social social social social social
social social social social social
arrival arrival arrival arrival arrival
arrival arrival arrival arrival arrival
original original original original
original original original original
professional professional professional
professional professional professional
unusual unusual unusual unusual
unusual unusual unusual unusual
authority authority authority
authority authority authority
auction auction auction auction
auction auction auction auction
extraordinary extraordinary
extraordinary extraordinary

extraordinary extraordinary
evaporate evaporate evaporate
evaporate evaporate evaporate
performance performance performance
performance performance performance
fortunate fortunate fortunate
fortunate fortunate fortunate
cherries cherries cherries cherries
cherries cherries cherries cherries
torches torches torches torches
torches torches torches torches
leaves leaves leaves leaves leaves
leaves leaves leaves leaves leaves
dresses dresses dresses dresses
dresses dresses dresses dresses
friends friends friends friends
friends friends friends friends
activities activities activities
activities activities activities
arches arches arches arches arches
arches arches arches arches arches
berries berries berries berries berries
berries berries berries berries berries

fairies fairies fairies fairies fairies
fairies fairies fairies fairies fairies
amount amount amount amount
amount amount amount amount
comic comic comic comic comic
comic comic comic comic comic
mountain mountain mountain
mountain mountain mountain
flour flour flour flour flour flour
flour flour flour flour flour flour
South South South South South
South South South South South
council council council council
council council council council
allow allow allow allow allow
allow allow allow allow allow
powder powder powder powder
powder powder powder powder
shower shower shower shower
shower shower shower shower
coward coward coward coward
coward coward coward coward
drowsy drowsy drowsy drowsy

drowsy drowsy drowsy drowsy
tower tower tower tower tower
tower tower tower tower tower
crowded crowded crowded crowded
crowded crowded crowded crowded
circus circus circus circus circus
circus circus circus circus circus
thirsty thirsty thirsty thirsty thirsty
thirsty thirsty thirsty thirsty thirsty
birthday birthday birthday birthday
birthday birthday birthday birthday
purchase purchase purchase purchase
purchase purchase purchase purchase
burglar burglar burglar burglar
burglar burglar burglar burglar
urgent urgent urgent urgent urgent
urgent urgent urgent urgent urgent
occurred occurred occurred occurred
occurred occurred occurred occurred
survive survive survive survive
survive survive survive survive
character character character
character character character

jewellery jewellery jewellery jewellery
jewellery jewellery jewellery jewellery
point point point point point point
point point point point point point
appoint appoint appoint appoint
appoint appoint appoint appoint
appointment appointment appointment
appointment appointment appointment
pointless pointless pointless pointless
pointless pointless pointless pointless
avoid avoid avoid avoid avoid
avoid avoid avoid avoid avoid
avoidable avoidable avoidable
avoidable avoidable avoidable
poison poison poison poison poison
poison poison poison poison poison
moist moist moist moist moist moist
moist moist moist moist moist moist
moisture moisture moisture moisture
moisture moisture moisture moisture
voice voice voice voice voice voice
voice voice voice voice voice voice
hoist hoist hoist hoist hoist hoist

hoist hoist hoist hoist hoist hoist

poise poise poise poise poise poise

poise poise poise poise poise poise

ointment ointment ointment ointment

ointment ointment ointment ointment

hare hare hare hare hare hare hare

hare hare hare hare hare hare hare

rare rare rare rare rare rare rare rare

rare rare rare rare rare rare rare rare

glare glare glare glare glare glare

glare glare glare glare glare glare

spare spare spare spare spare spare

spare spare spare spare spare spare

parents parents parents parents

parents parents parents parents

snare snare snare snare snare snare

snare snare snare snare snare

flare flare flare flare flare flare flare

flare flare flare flare flare flare flare

upstairs upstairs upstairs upstairs

upstairs upstairs upstairs upstairs

downstairs downstairs downstairs

downstairs downstairs downstairs

repair repair repair repair repair

repair repair repair repair repair

flair flair flair flair flair flair flair

flair flair flair flair flair flair flair

fairy fairy fairy fairy fairy fairy

fairy fairy fairy fairy fairy fairy

hairy hairy hairy hairy hairy hairy

hairy hairy hairy hairy hairy hairy

their their their their their their thei

their their their their their their thei

there there there there there there

there there there there there there

grown grown grown grown grown

grown grown grown grown grown

groan groan groan groan groan groa

groan groan groan groan groan

stationery stationery stationery

stationery stationery stationery

stationary stationary stationary

stationary stationary stationary

board board board board board boar

board board board board board boar

cymbal cymbal cymbal cymbal

cymbal cymbal cymbal cymbal
current current current current
current current current current
currant currant currant currant
currant currant currant currant
whether whether whether whether
whether whether whether whether
weather weather weather weather
weather weather weather weather
prays prays prays prays prays
prays prays prays prays prays
praise praise praise praise praise
praise praise praise praise praise
preys preys preys preys preys preys
preys preys preys preys preys preys
wherever wherever wherever
wherever wherever wherever
somewhere somewhere somewhere
somewhere somewhere somewhere
siren siren siren siren siren siren
siren siren siren siren siren siren
fireman fireman fireman fireman
fireman fireman fireman fireman

nature nature nature nature nature
nature nature nature nature nature
pleasure pleasure pleasure pleasure
pleasure pleasure pleasure pleasure
creature creature creature creature
creature creature creature creature
failure failure failure failure failure
failure failure failure failure failure
picture picture picture picture picture
picture picture picture picture picture
capture capture capture capture
capture capture capture capture
furniture furniture furniture furniture
furniture furniture furniture furniture
agriculture agriculture agriculture
agriculture agriculture agriculture
pasture pasture pasture pasture
pasture pasture pasture pasture
perishable perishable perishable
perishable perishable perishable
reasonable reasonable reasonable
reasonable reasonable reasonable
dependable dependable dependable

dependable dependable dependable
agreeable agreeable agreeable
agreeable agreeable agreeable
laughable laughable laughable
laughable laughable laughable
valuable valuable valuable valuable
valuable valuable valuable valuable
recognisable recognisable recognisable
recognisable recognisable recognisable
believable believable believable
believable believable believable
sensible sensible sensible sensible
sensible sensible sensible sensible
incredible incredible incredible
incredible incredible incredible
visible visible visible visible visible
visible visible visible visible visible
legible legible legible legible legible
legible legible legible legible legible
especially especially especially
especially especially especially
perform perform perform perform
perform perform perform perform

violent violent violent violent violent
violent violent violent violent violent
proud proud proud proud proud
proud proud proud proud proud
disagreement disagreement
disagreement disagreement
disagreement disagreement
excitement excitement excitement
excitement excitement excitement
observant observant observant
observant observant observant
innocent innocent innocent innocent
innocent innocent innocent innocent
reluctant reluctant reluctant reluctant
reluctant reluctant reluctant reluctant
assistant assistant assistant
assistant assistant assistant
confident confident confident
confident confident confident
hesitant hesitant hesitant hesitant
hesitant hesitant hesitant hesitant
pheasant pheasant pheasant
pheasant pheasant pheasant

sound sound sound sound sound
sound sound sound sound sound
our our our our our our our our
our our our our our our our our
hour hour hour hour hour hour
hour hour hour hour hour hour
towel towel towel towel towel towel
towel towel towel towel towel towel
power power power power power
power power power power power
individually individually individually
individually individually individually
physically physically physically
physically physically physically
armbands armbands armbands
armbands armbands armbands
balloon balloon balloon balloon
balloon balloon balloon balloon
blower blower blower blower blower
blower blower blower blower blower
bottle bottle bottle bottle bottle bottle
bottle bottle bottle bottle bottle bottle
create create create create create

create create create create create
creation creation creation creation
creation creation creation creation
deflate deflate deflate deflate deflate
deflate deflate deflate deflate deflate
fabric fabric fabric fabric fabric
fabric fabric fabric fabric fabric
hinge hinge hinge hinge hinge hinge
hinge hinge hinge hinge hinge hinge
imagination imagination imagination
imagination imagination imagination
inflatable inflatable inflatable
inflatable inflatable inflatable
lever lever lever lever lever lever
lever lever lever lever lever lever
monster monster monster monster
monster monster monster monster
pump pump pump pump pump pump
pump pump pump pump pump pump
push push push push push push
push push push push push push
squeeze squeeze squeeze squeeze
squeeze squeeze squeeze squeeze

syringe syringe syringe syringe
syringe syringe syringe syringe
tape tape tape tape tape tape tape
tape tape tape tape tape tape tape
tube tube tube tube tube tube tube
tube tube tube tube tube tube tube
tubing tubing tubing tubing tubing
tubing tubing tubing tubing tubing
tyre tyre tyre tyre tyre tyre tyre
tyre tyre tyre tyre tyre tyre tyre
whistle whistle whistle whistle
whistle whistle whistle whistle
symbol symbol symbol symbol
symbol symbol symbol symbol
symbolism symbolism symbolism
symbolism symbolism symbolism
symbolic symbolic symbolic symbolic
symbolic symbolic symbolic symbolic
system system system system
system system system system
systematic systematic systematic
systematic systematic systematic
systematically systematically

systematically systematically
systematically systematically
temperature temperature temperature
temperature temperature temperature
thorough thorough thorough
thorough thorough thorough
thoroughly thoroughly thoroughly
thoroughly thoroughly thoroughly
twelfth twelfth twelfth twelfth
twelfth twelfth twelfth twelfth
variety variety variety variety
variety variety variety variety
variable variable variable variable
variable variable variable variable
vegetable vegetable vegetable
vegetable vegetable vegetable
vehicle vehicle vehicle vehicle
vehicle vehicle vehicle vehicle
yacht yacht yacht yacht yacht
yacht yacht yacht yacht yacht
yachting yachting yachting yachting
yachting yachting yachting yachting